EYEWITNESS TO HISTORY

LAURA INGALLS WILDER

in her own words

Gareth Stevens
PUBLISHING

By
Kristen
Rajczak

Please visit our website, www.garethstevens.com. For a free color catalog of all our high-quality books, call toll free 1-800-542-2595 or fax 1-877-542-2596.

Library of Congress Cataloging-in-Publication Data

Rajczak, Kristen.
 Laura Ingalls Wilder in her own words / Kristen Rajczak.
     pages cm. — (Eyewitness to history)
 Includes bibliographical references and index.
 ISBN 978-1-4824-4070-6 (pbk.)
 ISBN 978-1-4824-4071-3 (6 pack)
 ISBN 978-1-4824-4072-0 (library binding)
 1. Wilder, Laura Ingalls, 1867-1957—Juvenile literature. 2. Authors, American—20th century—Biography—Juvenile literature. 3. Women pioneers—United States—Biography—Juvenile literature. 4. Children's stories—Authorship—Juvenile literature. I. Title.
 PS3545.I342Z825 2016
 813'.52—dc23
 [B]

                                          2015029225

First Edition

Published in 2016 by
Gareth Stevens Publishing
111 East 14th Street, Suite 349
New York, NY 10003

Copyright © 2016 Gareth Stevens Publishing

Designer: Katelyn E. Reynolds
Editor: Therese Shea

Photo credits: Cover, p. 1 (Laura Ingalls Wilder) Nard the Bard/Wikipedia.org; cover, pp. 1 (background image), 16–17 TimothyMN/Wikipeia.org; cover, p. 1 (logo quill icon) Seamartini Graphics Media/Shutterstock.com; cover, p. 1 (logo stamp) YasnaTen/Shutterstock.com; cover, p. 1 (color grunge frame) DmitryPrudnichenko/Shutterstock.com; cover, pp. 1–32 (paper background) Nella/Shutterstock.com; cover, pp. 1–32 (decorative elements) Ozerina Anna/Shutterstock.com; pp. 1–32 (wood texture) Reinhold Leitner/Shutterstock.com; pp. 1–32 (open book background) Elena Schweitzer/Shutterstock.com; pp. 1–32 (bookmark) Robert Adrian Hillman/Shutterstock.com; pp. 5, 23 Plum111/Wikipedia.org; pp. 6–7 Jodamiller/Wikipedia.org; p. 7 (top) Biedronka/Wikipedia.org; p. 9 David Knox/Hulton Archive/Getty Images; p. 11 Michael Ochs Archives/Getty Images; p. 13 (top) Cropbot/Wikipedia.org; p. 13 (bottom) NBC Television/courtesy of Getty Images; pp. 15, 25 courtesy of the Library of Congress; p. 19 Scisetti Alfio/Shutterstock.com; p. 19 (signature) Scewing/Wikipedia.org; p. 20 Jeff G./Wikipedia.org; p. 21 Arthur Griffin/The LIFE Picture Collection/Getty Images; p. 27 Julie Jordan Scott/Wikipedia.org; pp. 28–29 Uwe Dedering/Wikipedia.org.

Printed in the United States of America

CPSIA compliance information: Batch #CW16GS: For further information contact Gareth Stevens, New York, New York at 1-800-542-2595.

CONTENTS

Words in the glossary appear in **bold** type the first time they are used in the text.

PIONEER *Woman*

HARD WORK AND HOPE

Laura's writing is full of sayings that seem to instruct readers on leading a better life. Many encourage hard work: *"There is nothing wrong with God's plan that man should earn his bread by the sweat of his brow."* Others encourage **optimism**, such as *"Suffering passes while love is eternal"* and *"It is the sweet, simple things of life which are the real ones after all."* Both hard work and hope are major themes in Laura's books.

Laura Ingalls Wilder once wrote: *"It is not the things you have that make you happy. It is love and kindness and helping each other and just plain being good."* Laura was the author of one of the best-loved children's book series of all time, often known by the title of the third book in the series—*Little House on the Prairie*, or simply, the *Little House* books.

Laura described her books not as a *"history, but a true story founded on historical fact."* She wrote with great detail about growing up on the American frontier. To the millions of readers who have traveled to Wisconsin, Kansas, and beyond with her family, her stories serve as a great example of the American pioneer experience.

MORE TO KNOW

The Ingalls family was part of the movement of millions of US settlers heading west to find their fortune during the middle to late 1800s.

LITTLE HOUSE ON THE PRAIRIE

LAURA INGALLS WILDER

Though she drew upon her own experiences, Laura's books are fiction. However, many people have studied them and her life to learn what it was like to grow up as a pioneer.

The IMPORTANCE of Family

Laura Ingalls was born on February 7, 1867, in Wisconsin near the Mississippi River. Her parents, Charles and Caroline, had married in 1860 and already had one daughter, Mary, born in 1865. They lived in a cabin not far from the town of Pepin. Another girl, Carrie, was born in 1870, and 5 years later, Frederick Charles was born. Sadly, Freddy, as he was called, died as a baby. The final Ingalls daughter was born in 1877. They named her Grace.

MORE TO KNOW

When writing the *Little House* books, Laura would call the area around the cabin in Wisconsin the "Big Woods."

The *Little House* books wouldn't be the same without Laura's **depictions** of her family. However, the picture she painted was much rosier than reality. She left out her brother Freddy and his death altogether. She also greatly simplified her family's movements across the country.

6

In the Little House *books, Charles and Caroline Ingalls are simply called Pa and Ma.*

PA IN LIFE AND ON PAPER

Laura wrote in her book *The First Four Years,* *"Persons appear to us according to the light we throw upon them from our own minds."* Pa was a wonderful, caring father in his daughter's books. The real Charles ran away from his **debts** more than once and, to modern historians, seemed to act selfishly in moving the family around. Trying to make a living on the frontier was hard, though. Laura likely believed he was doing the best he could.

On THE MOVE

A childhood spent zigzagging across the frontier surely influenced Laura's belief in the value of having a place to call home. *"Home is the nicest word there is,"* she wrote.

MORE TO KNOW

The short time the Ingalls family lived in Kansas is the setting for *Little House on the Prairie.*

The Ingalls family lived in *"the little house in the big woods"* in Wisconsin until 1869. They then moved to Missouri with Caroline's brother and his family. The next year, Laura's uncle and cousins went back to Wisconsin. Charles Ingalls took his family to Kansas, having heard there was free land there for settlers.

The Ingalls soon found that the land in Kansas wasn't truly free. Where they chose to settle still belonged to the Osage tribe. These Native Americans were trying to keep the US government from forcing them off the land.

INDIAN TERRITORY

Native American tribes across the United States were being forced off their land by the US government throughout the 1800s. Pioneers feared the actions of tribes trying to protect their traditional homelands. Many felt settlers had a right to the land, though. In fact, Laura writes about this in *Little House on the Prairie*. A neighbor character says, *"Treaties or no treaties, the land belongs to folks that'll farm it. That's only common sense and justice."*

Like many pioneers, Laura and her family traveled by wagon.

As in the end of *Little House on the Prairie*, the Ingalls family left Kansas after being forced off Osage Indian land. In 1871, they moved back to the Big Woods of Wisconsin—they even lived in the same house! Laura used memories from this time period in *Little House in the Big Woods*: *"She was glad that the cozy house, and Pa and Ma and the firelight and the music, were now. They could not be forgotten, she thought, because now is now. It can never be a long time ago."*

In 1874, Charles moved his family to Walnut Grove, Minnesota. They tried to farm wheat, but 2 years in a row, grasshoppers destroyed the crops.

IOWA

One part of Laura's life wasn't used in her books at all. From 1876 to 1878, Charles and Caroline ran a hotel in Burr Oak, Iowa. The family had very little money and not many other options. Of this time, Laura wrote later that *"Ma was always tired; Pa was always busy."* It was a low time for the Ingalls family and certainly didn't fit Laura's hopeful tone in the *Little House* books.

A popular TV series based on Laura's books ran from 1974 to 1984. *Little House on the Prairie* was set in Walnut Grove and the characters were mostly based on those in her book *On the Banks of Plum Creek.* →

MORE TO KNOW

While many events in *Little House on the Prairie* actually happened to Laura's family, she was very young when her family lived on Osage land. It's unlikely she remembered their time in Kansas.

After 2 years in Iowa, the family moved back to Walnut Grove in 1878. Laura was 12, and to help support her family, she worked as a housekeeper and babysat for other families. But she wasn't in Walnut Grove long. The next year, Charles moved his family to De Smet, South Dakota. Laura grew to be a teenager there, working different jobs and eventually becoming a teacher at around 15 or 16. It was also around this time that Laura began to be **courted** by Almanzo Wilder.

Almanzo owned horses and was somewhat of a town hero for traveling to get supplies for everyone during a bad snowstorm. Almanzo called Laura "Bessie," and she called him "Manly." They were married in 1885 when Laura was 18.

MORE TO KNOW

Laura's jobs and teaching helped support her family. Her older sister was blind by this time, which in the *Little House* books was caused by an illness called scarlet fever. The cause was more likely measles or **meningitis**.

On the TV show, Almanzo was just a few years older than Laura. The real Almanzo was 10 years older than Laura, though.

One of Laura's books isn't about her family, but Almanzo's childhood on a New York farm. In *Farmer Boy*, the admiring Laura wrote: *"A farmer depends on himself, and the land and the weather. If you're a farmer, you raise what you eat, you raise what you wear, and you keep warm with wood out of your own timber. You work hard, but you work as you please, and no man can tell you to go or come."*

THOSE HARD
First Years

THE WILDER CHILDREN

The year after Almanzo and Laura married, they had a daughter they named Rose. In 1889, they had another child, a boy. However, he died 12 days after he was born—and that was only 2 weeks before their house burned down. Raising Rose would prove to be challenging for Laura—and Rose, too. Rose wrote in her journal that Mama Bess, as she called her, *"made me so miserable as a child that I never got over it."*

Even as towns became more established, life for families on the American frontier was challenging. Laura and Almanzo were no exception. They both suffered bad illnesses, and a stroke left Almanzo limping for the rest of his life. In 1889, their house burned down, leaving them with almost nothing.

Laura wrote about these hard years in *The First Four Years*, mixing them with thoughts about the pioneer experience. She wrote of *"the creed of her pioneer forefathers that 'it is better farther on'—only instead of farther on in space, it was farther on in time, over the horizon of years ahead instead of the far horizon of the west."*

She and Almanzo believed it was *"better farther on"* in time and space. They first moved to Spring Valley, Minnesota, and then to Westville, Florida.

MORE TO KNOW

The First Four Years is the final book included in the *Little House* series. However, Laura never finished it.

By the end of the 1800s, people were able to travel through much of the country by railroad, as the Wilder family did as they went east.

The Wilder family's life didn't get easier in Florida. They returned to De Smet briefly in 1894 before moving on again. The family then settled in Mansfield, Missouri. They built a house and farm there, naming it Rocky Ridge. Laura raised chickens and tended an apple orchard.

Still, the family often went hungry. Later in life, Rose would blame the poor condition of her teeth on not eating enough as a child. She didn't have nice clothing or shoes, either. Rose often complained

MORE TO KNOW

Rocky Ridge is still standing. About 40,000 people visit it every year.

Rocky Ridge was built in the Ozark Mountains. Companies were saying the land there was great for settlers, but the soil turned out to be rocky and somewhat hard to farm.

that her mother didn't trust her to do even small chores right. Almanzo's health never returned completely, which left Laura doing her household duties and some of his. Years later, Laura would proudly proclaim, *"What we accomplished was without help of any kind."*

EVERY ROSE HAS ITS THORN

Rose left home right after high school to work as a **telegraph** operator. She worked in San Francisco, California, became a writer, and married and then divorced in her 20s. She left behind her hard childhood and learned languages, traveled, and ate at fancy restaurants. Rose was able to give her parents money and build them a new house. However, the relationship between Rose and Laura didn't improve much with the distance or the help offered by Rose.

THE WRITING
Starts

WRITING LIFE

By the 1920s, Rose had been working as an author and journalist for many years. She'd written for magazines and done a lot of reporting from places all over the world including France, Armenia, and Iraq. She also had written celebrity biographies and served as a **ghostwriter**. But her style was thought to be **sensational** or even tasteless. Actor Charlie Chaplin, President Herbert Hoover, and businessman Henry Ford were all unhappy with how she described them.

Around 1911, Laura started writing a column for the *Missouri Ruralist*. As Mrs. A. J. Wilder, she wrote about farming, housekeeping, and marriage. Sometimes, she even wrote about politics. For years, she also contributed to *McCall's Magazine*, the *St. Louis Star*, and other publications. She used her experiences to inform her readers about country life.

In 1929, the stock market crashed and a period of economic hardship called the Great Depression began. It echoed across the country, and Laura and Almanzo again found themselves struggling. Rose may have been the one who encouraged her mother to sit down and write about her memories of growing up. So, in 1930, Laura began to write her **autobiography**.

MORE TO KNOW

Laura was a big part of keeping Rocky Ridge running. She said: *"The fact is that while there has been a good deal of discussion for and against women in business, farm women have always been business women, and I have never heard a protest."*

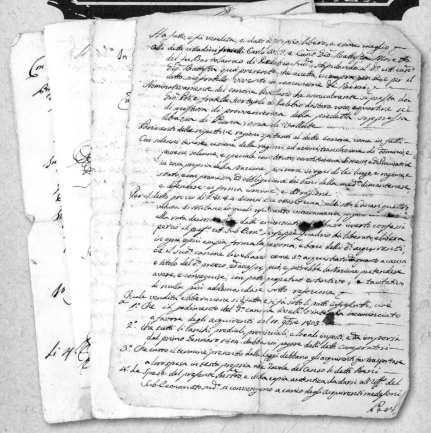

Laura is reported to have written out her autobiography.
She didn't type it.

Laura's actual signature:

Laura Ingalls Wilder

Laura called her autobiography *Pioneer Girl*. It followed her life from about age 3 to her marriage to Almanzo. She began sending it to agents and publishers, but no one wanted it. Like other industries, publishing had been badly affected by the Great Depression.

One editor who looked at *Pioneer Girl* thought it would be a good basis for a children's book, or "juvenile" as it was called then. That's when Rose stepped in. Laura wrote pages of a story while Rose typed them, shaping the story and taking it further from the truth. Rose wrote in a letter to her mother: *"A good bit of the detail that I add to your copy is for pure sensory effect."*

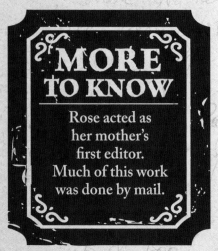

MORE TO KNOW

Rose acted as her mother's first editor. Much of this work was done by mail.

← *Rose Wilder*

Laura was the most likely author of the many small details that brought her series to life, such as how to make a rag doll.

FACT VS. FICTION

The final versions of the *Little House* books are a balancing act of Laura's memories and Rose's skillful dramatizing of events. Their conversation and occasional arguments over this play out in the many letters and **manuscript** notes between them. Laura once wrote to Rose: *"Even though these books must be made fit for children to read, they must also be true to history . . . I have given you a true picture of the times and the place and people. Please don't blur it."*

LITTLE HOUSE
in the Big Woods

AGE AND WISDOM

Laura was in her 60s when she started writing the *Little House* books. Her view of her life looking back is clear: *"As the years pass, I am coming more and more to understand that it is the common, everyday blessings of our common everyday lives for which we should be particularly grateful . . . just the pure air to breathe and the strength to breathe it; just warmth and shelter and home folks."*

Laura and Rose's efforts paid off. In 1932, *Little House in the Big Woods* was published. The fictional Laura is 4 years old and living in Wisconsin with her family. The book follows their life as they plant and harvest crops, search for food in winter, and celebrate Christmas. They tap maple trees for syrup and even make their own bullets. After each day's hard work, the family spends their evenings snugly together in their home.

The book was an immediate success. It was a runner-up for the famous children's literature honor, the Newbery Award. *The New York Times Book Review* praised Laura's story for having a *"refreshingly genuine and lifelike quality"* and said the character of Pa was *"drawn with loving care and reality."* Laura's publishers wanted another *Little House* book as soon as possible.

MORE TO KNOW

Laura's books have remained in print since they were first published.

Laura and Rose worked on the nine main Little House books over about 11 years.

LITTLE HOUSE IN THE BIG WOODS

LAURA INGALLS WILDER

ROSE'S *Contribution*

MORE TO KNOW

Even though Laura's books were a success, she said being an author was more important to her than the money she earned.

Many people today believe the *Little House* series was as much a product of Rose's creative editing as her mother's writing. In fact, Laura recognized her daughter's ability to make what she had written better. In a letter to Rose about the fourth book, *On the Banks of Plum Creek*, Laura wrote, *"I have written you the whys of the story as I wrote it, but you know your judgment is better than mine, so what you decide is the one that stands."*

Letters show how Rose was trying to teach her mother to work more independently, even early on in Laura's writing. In 1925, Rose wrote: *"You must understand that what sold was your article, edited. You must study how it was edited, and why."*

ROSE'S BOOKS

Rose wrote her own books about the pioneer experience, including *Let the Hurricane Roar*. It was first published in pieces in a magazine and then as a book in 1933. The name was later changed to *Young Pioneers* in 1976. Also based on the experiences of Charles and Caroline Ingalls, *Young Pioneers* was made into a TV movie and short-lived series not long after *Little House on the Prairie* began to air.

Though Rose (above) is sometimes credited with reworking Laura's **memoir** into a children's book, it's hard to know exactly how much is Rose's work and how much is Laura's.

LAURA'S *Legacy*

Collections of Laura's other writings were also published after her death. Diary entries she wrote during her, Almanzo, and Rose's trip from South Dakota to Missouri and a series of letters she wrote when visiting Rose in California in 1915 came out as books in the 1970s. Essays and columns she wrote about family, pioneer life, and being a woman were also gathered and made into books, too.

Laura died at age 90 in 1957. Her *Little House* books had won five Newbery Honors in the 1930s and 1940s and brought her success and fame. After her death, the manuscript of the unfinished book *The First Four Years* was found, along with mentions of Laura's writing of it in a letter to Rose: *"I thought it might **wangle** a little more advertising for the [Little House] books if I said I might write the grown up one."* She mentioned that Rose might put *her* name on it instead, if she could *"polish it."*

The book was published in 1971, unedited, and under Laura's name as the final *Little House* book. However, it's considered inferior to the earlier books.

Almanzo died at age 92 in 1949, and Rose died at 81 in 1968. All the Wilders are buried near Rocky Ridge in Mansfield, Missouri.

MORE TO KNOW

Today, the Laura Ingalls Wilder Award is given to a children's author each year.

WILDER

ALMANZO JAMES
1857—1949
LAURA INGALLS
1867—1957

Eighty-two years after *Little House in the Big Woods* was first published, a new book written by Laura Ingalls Wilder surprised *Little House* enthusiasts. In 2014, the South Dakota Historical Society Press published *Pioneer Girl*, the original autobiography Laura wrote! It includes maps and **annotations** by an editor as well as Laura's notes. Though there have been many biographies written about her, *Pioneer Girl* tells the true story of Laura's life to the public for the first time in her own words.

MORE TO KNOW

In 2008, a musical based on the *Little House* books opened. It starred Melissa Gilbert, the woman who portrayed Laura on the long-running TV show, as Caroline Ingalls.

Written for adults, the book paints a much grimmer picture of pioneer life than the *Little House* books and includes violence, sickness, and death. For lovers of Laura's children's books, *Pioneer Girl* is an opportunity to peek behind the curtain of fiction to find the real history of a beloved author.

THE MANY TRAVELS
OF LAURA
INGALLS WILDER

Spring Valley, MN
1890–1891

De Smet, SD
1879–1890
1892–1894

Pepin, WI
1867–1869
1871–1874

Walnut Grove, MN
1874–1876
1878–1879

Burr Oak, IA
1876–1878

Osage Territory, KS
1869–1871

Mansfield, MO
1894–1957

Westville, FL
1891–1892

*Follow Laura's travels around
the United States using this map.*

CONTINUED SUCCESS

Laura wrote: *"As you read my stories of long ago I hope you will remember that things truly worthwhile and that will give you happiness are the same now as they were then."* People all over the world have enjoyed seeing the world of pioneers through young Laura's eyes. *Little House in the Big Woods* alone has sold more than 60 million copies and has been published in 33 languages. It remains an introduction to this important American pioneer period.

GLOSSARY

annotation: a note of explanation added to a book

autobiography: the story of someone's life written by that person

court: to try to gain another's interest

debt: an amount of money owed

depiction: a description using words and stories

ghostwriter: someone who writes something for or with somebody else with the other person receiving credit as the author

manuscript: the original copy of a book before it's published

memoir: a written account of someone's past experiences

meningitis: a serious, sometimes fatal illness with symptoms such as severe headaches, vomiting, stiff neck, and high fever

optimism: a feeling or belief that good things will happen in the future

sensational: putting too much stress on the most shocking parts of something

telegraph: a way of sending messages over a long distance using wires and electrical signals

wangle: to get something using indirect methods

FOR MORE
Information

Books

Leaf, Christina. *Laura Ingalls Wilder*. Minneapolis, MN: Bellwether Media, 2016.

McDonough, Yona Zeldis. *Little Author in the Big Woods: A Biography of Laura Ingalls Wilder*. New York, NY: Christa Ottaviano Books, 2014.

Wilder, Laura Ingalls. *Little House in the Big Woods*. New York, NY: HarperCollins Publishers, 2007.

Websites

American Pioneers
www.selah.k12.wa.us/soar/projects2000/pioneerweb/trail.html
Learn more about what pioneer life was like for Laura and her family.

Laura Ingalls Wilder Historic Home & Museum
www.lauraingallswilderhome.com
You can visit Laura's home in Missouri where she wrote the books about her life as a pioneer.

INDEX